ANCIENT EGYPT

DISCOVERIES & INVENTIONS

JANE SHUTER

First published in Great Britain by Heinemann Library
Halley Court, Jordan Hill, Oxford OX2 8EJ
a division of Reed Educational and Professional Publishing Ltd.
Heinemann is a registered trademark of Reed Educational & Professional Publishing Limited.

OXFORD MELBOURNE AUCKLAND KUALA LUMPUR
SINGAPORE IBADAN NAIROBI KAMPALA
JOHANNESBURG GABORONE PORTSMOUTH NH CHICAGO

Designed by Clare Sleven
Illustrations by Jonathan Adams, Jeff Edwards
Printed in Hong Kong

02 01 00 99 98
10 9 8 7 6 5 4 3 2 1

ISBN 0 431 00494 3

British Library Cataloguing in Publication Data

Shuter, Jane
Egypt : discoveries and inventions. - (Ancient world topic books)
1 . Discoveries in science - Egypt - History - Juvenile literature 2 . Egypt - Religion - Juvenile literature 3 . Egypt - History - To 332 B. C. - Juvenile literature
I . Title
932

Acknowledgements

The Publishers would like to thank the following for permission to reproduce photographs: AKG Photo: p11; Ancient Art & Architecture Collection: pp10, 17, 23; British Museum: p14; Committee of Egypt Exploration p18, Michael Holford: p15; Middle East Pictures: C Osborne p5; R Scruton p29; Wellcome Centre Medical Photographic Library p19; Werner Forman Archive: pp16, 21

Cover photograph reproduced with permission of R Sheridan, Ancient Art & Architecture Collection

Any words appearing in the text in bold, **like this**, are explained in the Glossary.

CONTENTS

INTRODUCTION

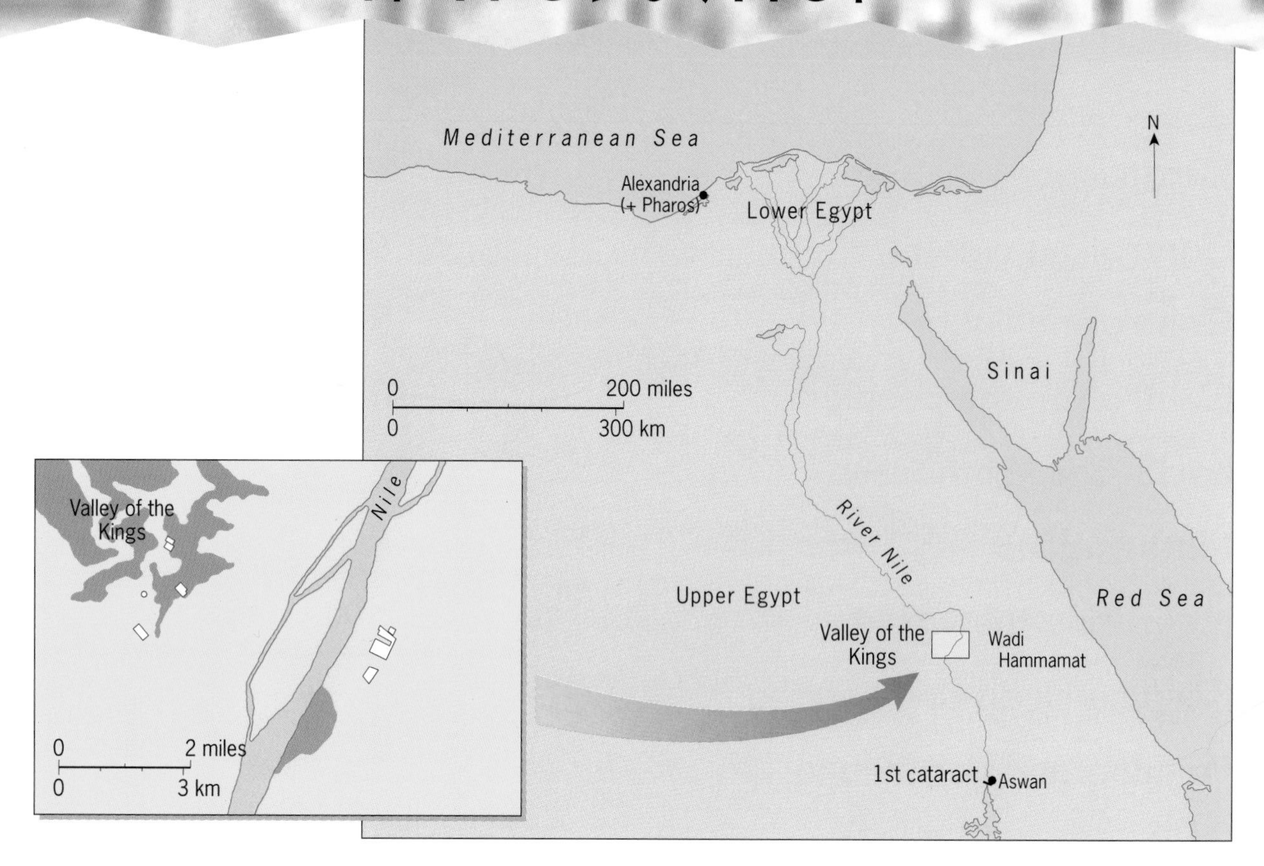

This chart shows different times in the long history of Ancient Egypt. The red blocks show when **pharaohs** were weak and no one ran the whole country.

The Ancient Egyptians lived a long time ago, but many of their inventions are familiar to us. Some of them, such as locks, were forgotten and had to be invented again. Other things, such as calendars, have been handed down to us through other peoples who used them, like the Greeks.

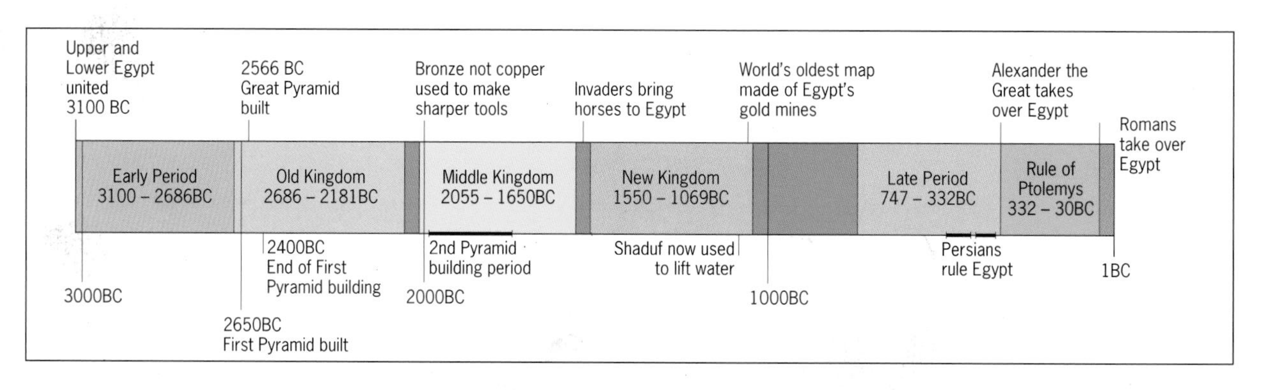

THEN AND NOW

The Ancient Egyptians measured years and hours as we do now. People wore make-up and used umbrellas (they were keeping off the sun, not the rain). Their houses had bathrooms and toilets. This does not mean that the Ancient Egyptians were just like people now. There were lots of ways in which they were very different. But 2000 years ago you would have felt more at home in Egypt than you would in Britain.

Today, farmers still use an Ancient Egyptian invention, the shaduf, to lift water from the river. It was invented during the New Kingdom.

Egypt is a hot, dry, **desert** land. The only place people could grow crops was in the thick mud left behind after the River Nile flooded each year. The difference between the Red Land (desert) and the Black Land (the mud left by the river) was so clear that a person could stand with a foot on each.

Crops planted in Egypt needed watering every day. So the Egyptians had to control the water. They used ponds and **ditches** with wooden **sluices** to hold back water and move it around the fields.

CANALS

In about 2400BC Uni, governor of Upper Egypt, had a **canal** built to go around the waterfalls where the River Nile changed level at Aswan. Boats could then go further up the Nile than ever before. The Ancient Egyptians also built a canal joining the Nile and the Red Sea. The canal was finished by 1470BC. It needed a lot of repairing, even rebuilding, over the years.

We know there was a canal between the Nile and the Red Sea, across the desert, in 1470BC. Carvings at Queen Hatshepsut's **temple** show her ships travelling through it.

One of the ways we can find out about the Ancient Egyptians is to study the paintings in their tombs. The **tombs** were dug deep into the rock. How did they see to paint? Did they light the tombs in the same way that they lit their mines for digging up gold and precious stones?

USING THE SUN

Archaeologists investigating an Ancient Egyptian mine in Sinai found some tools left behind with some pieces of **bronze** mirrors. They think mirrors were used to reflect the outside sunlight down, deep into the mines. They could have done this in tombs, too. Some guides in the tombs today reflect light down from outside to show people around.

LAMPS AND TORCHES

When it was impossible to reflect sunlight, the Ancient Egyptians used pottery torches. A twisted linen string was burned in oil or animal fat mixed with salt. The salt stopped the burning oil or fat from smoking. Smoke would have spoiled the paintings.

Tomb painters at work. They built platforms to reach the tops of the walls. Sometimes they painted the ceilings, too.

The **pharaohs** kept a tight hold on the people of Ancient Egypt. They made sure they paid their **taxes**, obeyed the laws and did their **corvée** – the yearly work they had to do for the pharaoh.

KEEPING TRACK

To make sure that no one was cheating, the pharaoh's **scribes** kept records of the taxes paid and the work done. They checked past records to see how much land people had, and how much tax they had paid before.

Scribes kept their records on rolls of paper made from papyrus reeds. They worked sitting crossed-legged.

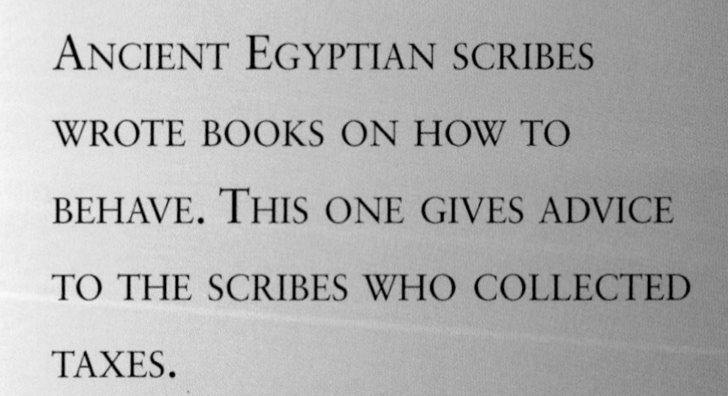

ANCIENT EGYPTIAN SCRIBES WROTE BOOKS ON HOW TO BEHAVE. THIS ONE GIVES ADVICE TO THE SCRIBES WHO COLLECTED TAXES.

Do not make the worker wretched by taking too much tax. Leave him well off, then he will work the land and pay taxes next year. If you take too much tax he will run away.

POLICE

Scribes did not chase criminals or people who cheated. There were various kinds of police to do that. We know that Ancient Egypt had a police force by 2500BC. It made sure that people paid their taxes and obeyed the laws.

By 1320BC, there were several kinds of police. As well as ordinary police, there were river police to catch the pirates that attacked boats on the River Nile. There were police to guard gold mines and police to guard the important **tombs** in the Valley of the Kings. The police force became more organized and many policemen came from the same families.

Policemen punish a man for not paying his taxes.

LOCKS

Ancient Egyptian doors were made of wood. They have long since rotted away. At first, people thought that the Ancient Egyptians may not have had doors or window shutters at all, let alone locks. But they did. **Archaeologists** now think the Egyptians first made very simple locks using wooden pegs and string. Then they invented much more complicated wooden locks. In these locks the key was like a toothbrush with several wooden 'bristles'. These bristles matched holes inside the lock. Only the right key could open the lock. This system is like the one Yale keys use today.

THE WORLD'S FIRST LIGHTHOUSE

The world's first lighthouse was built in 270BC, on the island of Pharos, which faced the port of Alexandria. It was built for the **pharaoh** Ptolemy II. It was made to guide ships into the harbour, but also to show how very powerful Ancient Egypt was.

The lighthouse at Alexandria. It is joined to the city of Alexandria by a raised road.

To build huge buildings like the lighthouse at Pharos, or the pyramids, the Ancient Egyptians needed to be able to work things out exactly. One of the papyrus paper scrolls that has survived from the time is full of ways to work out angles, heights and distances. The Egyptians used maths to make sure the huge buildings they built did not fall or lean over. Maths helped them make huge statues to the right scale so that they still looked like people.

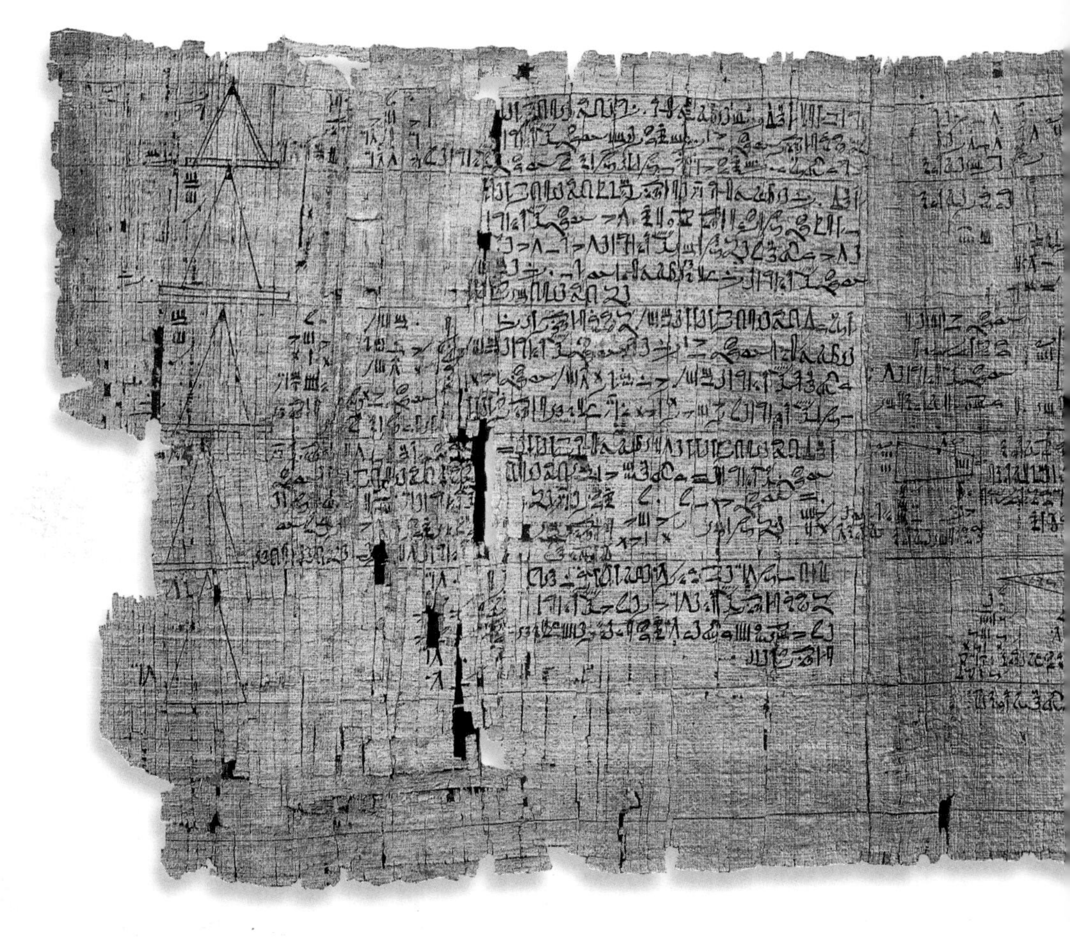

Part of the Rhind Mathematical Papyrus. These calculations are to do with pyramids.

The scribes working in this picture are counting all the geese on an estate. It was impossible to count every animal, even when they were in cages. The scribe on the left has a measure and is working out the number of geese mathematically.

EVERYDAY MATHS

Mathematics was not only useful to builders. **Scribes** were trained to do maths, too. If they ran a village or an **estate** they needed to be able to work out the **taxes** on **crops**, as well as write everything down.

MATHEMATICAL PAPYRUS SCROLLS TAUGHT SCRIBES HOW TO DEAL WITH REAL-LIFE SITUATIONS, TOO. THE RHIND PAPYRUS HAS EXAMPLES OF THE PROBLEMS A SCRIBE RUNNING A VILLAGE WOULD HAVE.

Fat worth 10 gallons of grain has been given you for the year. How much fat can you use each day?

Can 10 gallons of grain be stored in a granary bin that is 5 cubits long, 5 cubits wide and 5 cubits deep?

The Ancient Egyptians had rulers for ordinary measurements. These rods measured cubits (the distance from a man's elbow to the end of his middle finger). Cubits were broken up into smaller measures, the smallest being a finger wide.

MAPPING THINGS OUT

The Egyptians were the first to make detailed maps of places and of the stars in the sky. Most sky maps were made by priests, to work out when to hold **religious ceremonies**. The priests worked out the difference between the stars and the planets. They knew about five of the planets: Mars, Saturn, Jupiter, Venus and Mercury.

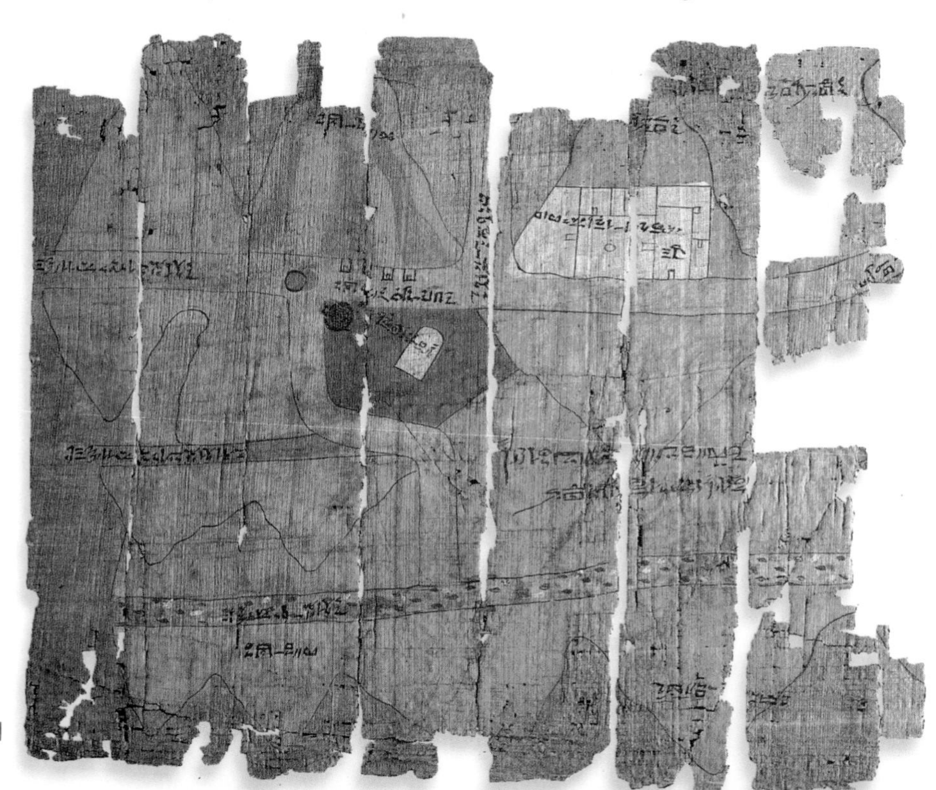

This is the earliest map that has been found. It shows the Wadi Hammamat gold mines. It is from about 1150BC.

MEASURING TIME

The Egyptians used water clocks to tell the time. Water drained out of a jar marked in 12 'hour' sections. Hours were of different lengths in the summer and winter. There had to be 12 hours of darkness and 12 of light in each day, and there was less light in the winter days. The Egyptians used a 365-day calendar for the year, as we do. They also made calendars with carefully worked out lucky and unlucky days marked on them. They believed in magic, so tried not to do important things on the unlucky days.

This **tomb** decoration shows the gods and goddesses of Egypt and various groups of stars.

Ancient Egyptians believed in keeping clean. They washed themselves and their clothes every day. But water was precious so they had to use as little as possible. They washed clothes in the river. They did not have deep baths. The bath water was drained off into a stone jar to be taken to water the fields.

TOILETS

The Ancient Egyptians had toilets, but no drains. Again, this was probably to save water. Toilets were pottery bowls with stone or wooden seats. They were emptied every few days on to the fields as **fertilizer**.

A limestone toilet seat, the only seat to have survived from Ancient Egypt. Only rich people would have a stone seat – wood was more common.

These carvings show a doctor's surgical instruments.

DOCTORS

Egyptian doctors treated their patients with a mixture of magic and medicine. They would say a spell over the patient as they treated them. Both parts of the treatment had to work to cure the patient.

SEVERAL EGYPTIAN MEDICAL PAPYRUS PAPER SCROLLS HAVE SURVIVED UP TO THE PRESENT. THEY SHOW HOW DOCTORS USED MAGICAL SPELLS WITH MEDICINE. HERE IS ONE SPELL.

Come! You who drive evil things from my stomach and my limbs! He who drinks this medicine shall be cured, just as the gods above were cured.
An Egyptian doctor wrote next to this spell, 'This spell is really good – successful many times'.

Artists could not just paint what they wanted. There were rules about how people should look – how they stood or sat and how big they were. These rules were passed down over many years. The **tomb** owner was shown as the biggest person. Servants were painted so small, they look like children. There were also rules about the colour of people. Men had to have darker skin than women.

COLOURS

The Egyptians were the first people to make some colours (such as blue) by mixing chemicals rather than using 'natural' dyes, like dyes from plants. Blue was used for the sky and for the skins of sky gods and goddesses. Different colours had different meanings. Black was the colour of death and preservation. This is why **mummies** are shown as black. Green was used to show coming back to life. Osiris, when shown as god of the afterlife, has a green face.

1 The first sketches are done in red, to make sure everything fits on the wall.

2 The red sketches are corrected in black.

3 The carvers carve out the black sketches.

4 They cover the wall in a layer of water and chalk.

Some of the walls of tombs were unfinished, so we can see all the stages of the work. These carvings come from the tomb of the **pharaoh** Horemheb.

5 The painters then paint the wall – the finished **hieroglyphs**.

THE FIRST ZOO?

The first zoo was probably set up by the **pharaoh** Thutmose III (1479–1425BC), who made a huge collection of animals and plants from other countries. Rulers of countries controlled by Ancient Egypt sent him strange animals as part of their 'tribute', or **tax**. Lots of **tombs** have pictures of collecting the tribute from various countries. The paintings on the tomb wall of Thutmose's chief adviser, Rekhmire, show strange animals as tributes – elephants, a bear and a giraffe.

THE LAST EGYPTIAN ZOO

One of the last pharaohs, Ptolemy II, had a huge zoo built at Alexandria. (It was Ptolemy II who had the world's first lighthouse built.) His zoo was the biggest in the world and had lions, leopards and other wild cats, elephants, buffaloes, a rhino, snakes, parrots and even a polar bear!

Some of the animals sent as tribute to the pharaoh Thutmose III.

The Ancient Egyptians developed two sorts of writing: **hieroglyphs** and **hieratic**. Hieratic was a simple form of hieroglyphs used for everyday writing, such as for letters and **accounts**.

HIEROGLYPHS

Hieroglyphs were complicated. At first, people drew pictures of what they wanted to say, so a picture of an owl meant 'an owl'. But then pictures were used to show some sounds. They showed the first sound of the word. The Egyptian for owl began with a 'm'. So a picture of an owl came to mean the sound 'm'.

Only 27 sounds had a hieroglyph. Some sounds did not have one. So sometimes a set of hieroglyphs could mean three or four different words, depending on what the missing sounds were. The Ancient Egyptians did not find this confusing – they just added a picture hieroglyph for the whole word.

MAKING PAPER

Scribes practised writing on boards which could be painted over and used again. But important records and books were written on long paper scrolls. The paper was made from papyrus reeds which grew along the river. The reeds were sliced into strips, beaten flat, then laid over each other in layers. The layers were pressed together between heavy stones to make one sheet of papyrus. This was joined to other sheets to make a long strip, which was then polished with a smooth stone.

CLOTHES

Most clothes in Ancient Egypt were made out of linen. This was made from **flax**, which grew well all over the country. Rich and poor people wore the same simple tunic-style of clothes. Rich people wore thinner cloth, which was more expensive.

WIGS

Most Ancient Egyptians shaved their hair off or wore it very short, because of the heat. For special occasions people wore wigs made either of wool or human hair. Some hair wigs still had head lice from the original owner!

DRESSING UP

Even rich people usually dressed simply. But they dressed up on special occasions. Both men and women wore jewellery and perfume. They both wore make-up, too. They wore kohl eyeliner. The natural disinfectant in **kohl** helped stop eye infections, while the eyeliner looked good. They also wore coloured eye shadow, and red-ochre powder mixed with fat on their lips.

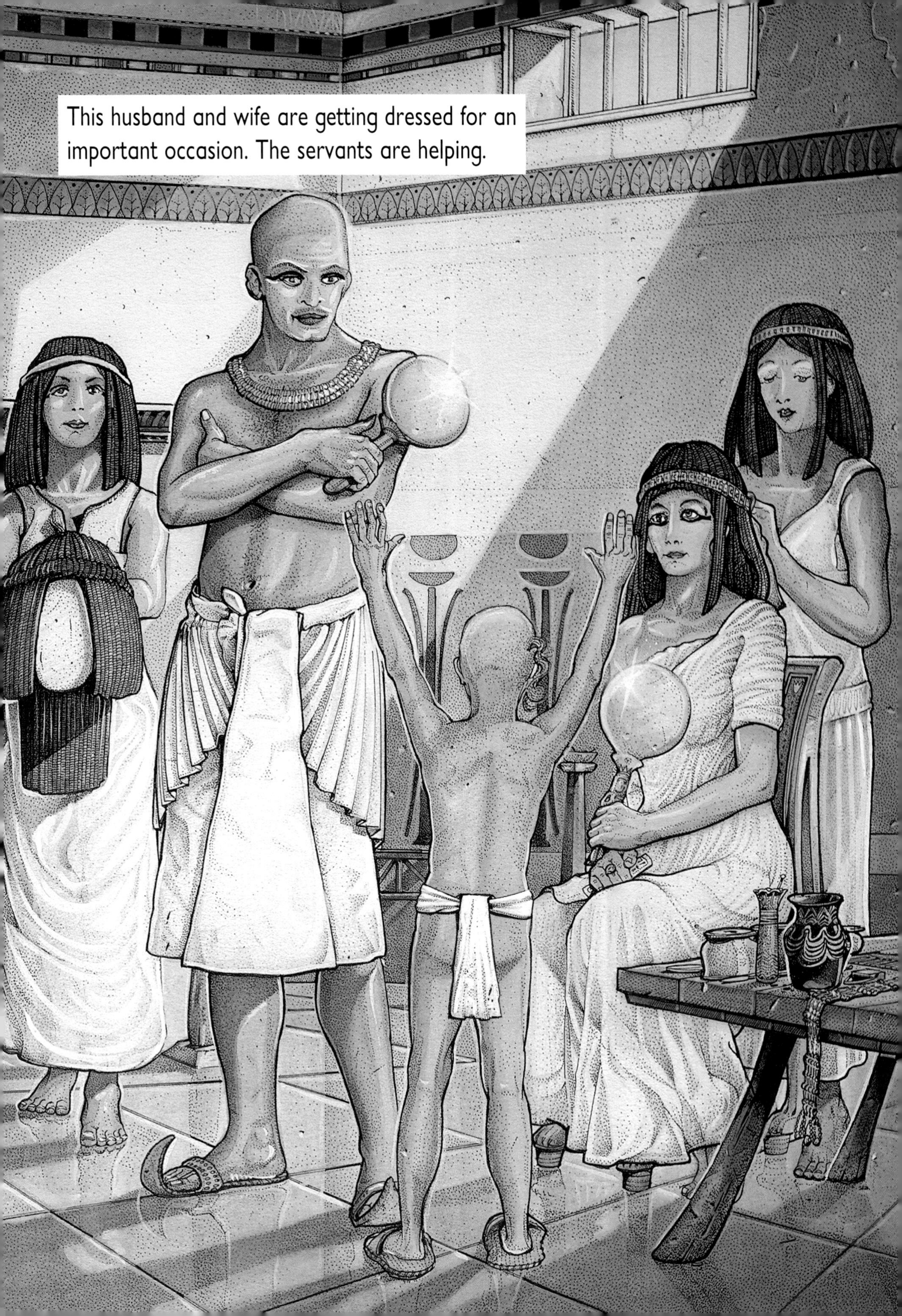

This husband and wife are getting dressed for an important occasion. The servants are helping.

HOW DO WE KNOW WHAT THEY KNEW?

EVIDENCE FROM THE TIME

Most of the evidence that tells us about what the Ancient Egyptians knew comes from special scrolls. These were written at the time to teach new **scribes**.

We can also look at **tomb paintings** and writings by people who visited Ancient Egypt. Many huge buildings and statues that the Egyptians made are still standing today.

A GREEK WRITER VISITED EGYPT IN ABOUT 450BC. HE WROTE ABOUT SOME EGYPTIAN DISCOVERIES.

The Egyptians, by studying the stars, discovered the solar year. So they were the first to divide the year into twelve parts. In my opinion, this is much better than the Greek way. They have twelve months of thirty days each and need only to add five days to each year for the regular circle of the seasons. We Greeks need to add a full month each year in our way of working.

NEW EVIDENCE

Archaeologists and scientists have used chemical analysis and x-rays to find out about Ancient Egyptian paints and dyes. This is how they found out that 'Egyptian blue' was the first chemical, not natural, dye. It was made by heating copper salts, calcium and sand to over 700°C (water boils at 100°C).

Experts at Bristol University examined the **mummy** case of Horemkenesi. They found out how the colours that were used to paint it were made. They also worked out the order in which the colours were painted on.

accounts lists of all the crops and other things that a person owned, as well as where they were stored and when they were used

archaeologists people who dig up and study things left behind from past times

bronze a metal made by heating and mixing copper and tin

canal a deep ditch, filled with water, built to take ships from one place to another

corvée all Egyptians who were not scribes had to do this work on the pharaoh's land for a set number of days each year

desert a dry place which has little or no rain all year

ditch a ditch is long and narrow, dug out around a piece of land to trap water draining off it or take water to it

estate a large piece of land with homes and farmland, all run by the same person

fertilizer something that adds things to the soil to help plants grow better

flax blue-flowered plant. Its seed make oil and its stems make linen thread.

hieratic a simple form of hieroglyphs, used for letters and ordinary writing jobs

hieroglyphs Egyptian picture writing

kohl a mixture of natural substances which was used in make-up

mummies bodies of dead people that have been preserved
pharaoh the king who ruled Egypt
religious ceremonies special times when people go to one place to pray to a god or goddess
scribes the only people in Ancient Egypt who could read and write. Scribes ran the country for the pharaoh.
sluice a board across a ditch that can be lifted or shut to let water out or hold it in
tax a payment that you have to make to whoever is running the country
temple a place where gods and goddesses are worshipped
tomb a place where someone is buried
tomb models tiny carvings or pottery shapes of people and things that were put in tombs
tomb paintings paintings on the walls of tombs

INDEX